Relentless Mercy

A Sermonic Commentary on Jonah

John M. Burris

Copyright © 2025 John M. Burris

All rights reserved.

No part of this book may be reproduced, stored in a retrieval system, or transmitted by any means, electronic, mechanical, photocopying, recording, or otherwise, without written permission from the author.

ISBN (Paperback): 979-8-9921204-7-9
ISBN (eBook): 979-8-9921204-6-2

Dedication

To Mom and Dad, Jim and Sue Salles. As Naomi did for Ruth, you have done for me. Even before you lost a child, you took me into your family as one of your own and I am forever grateful.

To my precious bride Jenny, you are everything I'm not to the greatest extreme in the best ways possible. Your patience, servanthood, and faithfulness have met my fears, sickness, and despair when I needed it most.

To my children, Jenna and Jackson, I am amazed at the way each of you serves and follows Jesus. Your faith is your own and it is real! I am so proud of both of you.

And most of all to my Abba Father, "It is He who reveals the profound and hidden things; He knows what is in the darkness, And the light dwells with Him."—Daniel 2:22

Table of Contents

Preface vii

Running From God—Jonah 1:1—3 1

From Prophet to Castaway—Jonah 1:4—16 13

A Cry from the Depths—Jonah 1:17—2:10 24

The Great City Repents—Jonah 3:1—10 37

The Reflection of the Heart—Jonah 4:1—11 49

One more thing… 63

For Further Study 67

Preface

During an interim period at the church I serve, I had the opportunity to fill in for five weeks in a row. In my position as Associate Pastor, I usually only get one week (most often a holiday) or two at best. I was excited for the opportunity to tackle a larger portion of Scripture and build on it week by week. I arrived at the book of Jonah quickly. I'd like to say I had a significant moment in prayer when God spoke clearly that I was to choose the book of Jonah for my text. In reality, it was more that it had four chapters, and I could use the first week as an introduction and background message.

With Jonah set to be my text, I began to gather commentaries, read articles, watch sermons by other pastors, and read and re-read the text repeatedly. I was captivated. In my thirty-four years of ministry, I had never done a message or even a Bible study on Jonah. I had referred to the book, and read the book several times but usually in conjunction with an attempt to read through the Bible in a year where I must admit the goal was finishing, not studying.

What I discovered was a treasure of epic proportions. Most of all, I discovered that I am Jonah. It was a soul-searching summer I spent in preparation for the five-week series. Jonah is far deeper than his journey to the depths of the sea. Jonah is not a story about a whale or a fable of a runaway prophet. The book of Jonah is a real account of a man who was flawed and conflicted, just like us. Most of all, the book of Jonah is about a God of Relentless Mercy who has compassion on people who don't know Him and infinite lovingkindness for those who do know Him, even if they are as far from Him as Tarshish.

I didn't change much from my weekly sermon manuscripts for this book. I wanted it to be useable, so it reads like a sermon. But I hope there is enough scholarship to help you navigate the complexities of a well—crafted account of The Relentless Mercy of God.

John M. Burris
Kingwood, Texas

Running From God
Jonah 1:1—3

What do you do when God tells you something that you don't want to hear?

Maybe it's "you're going to move across the country, or the world with your job" or "I want you to leave your career and go into ministry full time" or "I want you to go and make things right with the person you are at odds with" or even harder, "I want you to humble yourself and receive the correction of a brother or sister in Christ" or maybe it's a diagnosis that comes and you realize that you're going to have to walk through the disease to whatever end it brings.

For me it was a trip to the Emergency Room in December of 2023 for what I thought was just a kidney stone or bladder infection. After blood work and scans, the ER doctor very nervously delivered the news that I had a massive tumor on my right kidney. The news almost took my breath away. My mother died of kidney cancer in 2015 so the news was just as good as a death sentence to me.

Two surgeries later, one to remove my right kidney and one to remove my left adrenal gland, and the beginning of a two-year regimen of immunotherapy has given me hope that the Lord has much more in store for me. But, along the way my faith has wavered like never before. For those of you who have been through this (and are going through it), it is a journey that none of us would wish on anyone.

But what I have learned about the Lord through this I would never have learned otherwise. My diagnosis and journey have made me test the mettle of the faith I thought I had.

Make no mistake, we all want to call our own shots. Many of us treat God like some kind of divine genie who is just there to make our lives go the way we want. How many of our prayers are filled with, "God do this for me", "God this is hard make it easier", "God get me out of this situation."

The hardest place in your life to be is in the hands of God, totally at His mercy.

Think about it. We all make plans, and we find security in that. We have a mental image of our ideal lives, and we go after that. And if God chooses to get on board with us and help us realize our reality then all the better. But I wonder, how many of us could honestly say that we have completely yielded our whole life into the hands of God?

Well, we are going to witness first-hand what happens to the prophet Jonah as he wrestles with these kinds of issues. Let me just set the stage with some background:

- **The period**—approximately. 760 B.C. This happens after King David and after Israel has divided into Northern and Southern Kingdoms. Jeroboam is King of the Northern Kingdom of Israel during this time. Remember that after David and then Solomon, the people of God are led by many different kings most of whom don't follow the Lord. Jeroboam was one of those Kings who did not follow the Lord's commands. Consequently, around forty years after the time of Jonah, in 722 BC, the Northern Kingdom of Israel is taken captive by the Assyrians (more about them in a minute). Jonah is a contemporary of the prophet Elisha, coming just behind the prophet Elijah.
- **The book**—There are some scholars who treat the book as an allegory and the events described in the book are just there to teach and they didn't really happen. Let me give you two quick reasons why I strongly deny that opinion. 1.) Jonah, as we have seen is referred to in the book of 2 Kings 14:25 as a real prophet of God under King Jeroboam II (ca.

793—758 BC) 2.) Jesus Himself refers to Jonah in Matthew 12:40 and Luke 11:30. *"for just as Jonah was three days and three nights in the belly of the sea monster, so will the Son of Man be three days and three nights in the heart of the earth."* One other interesting note is that the Jews read the book of Jonah every year on the Day of Atonement.

- **The prophet**—As I mentioned, Jonah is referred to in 2 Kings as a prophet under King Jeroboam II. We also learn from that verse that he was from Gath—Hepher (GATH—HEE—fur). Gath—Hepher is in Galilee in the territory of the tribe of Zebulun and scholars place it near Nazareth, the town of Jesus' childhood. Jewish tradition holds that Jonah is believed to be the son of the widow from Zarephath, the boy who Elijah raised from the dead in 1 Kings 17, but I wouldn't put much stock into that. Jonah's name means "dove" which in the Bible a dove is pictured as a messenger or a symbol of foolishness. We will see throughout our study that both apply to Jonah.
- **The setting**—while some of the action in the book takes place elsewhere, the main location involved is the city of Nineveh. We find Nineveh all the way back in Genesis 10 in the Bible where it is described

as a city built by Nimrod. Nineveh was in Assyria, modern-day Mosul, Iraq. Four times in the book of Jonah, Nineveh is called a "great" city. What is meant is that Nineveh is a vast and powerful city, not great as in desirable. The prophet Nahum gives a description of the brutal landscape of Nineveh in Nahum 3:1—3.

Woe to the bloody city, completely full of lies and pillage;
Her prey never departs.
² The noise of the whip,
The noise of the rattling of the wheel,
Galloping horses
And bounding chariots!
³ Horsemen charging,
Swords flashing, spears gleaming,
Many slain, a mass of corpses,
And countless dead bodies—
They stumble over the dead bodies!

Ancient depictions of Assyrians show a pile of decapitated heads and soldiers skinning their captives. It is important to mention the brutality of Nineveh when we consider Jonah's reluctance to go there.

With all that in mind, let's go to the text and look at just the first three verses of chapter 1.

The word of the Lord came to Jonah the son of Amittai saying, ² "Arise, go to Nineveh the great city and cry against it, for their wickedness has come up before Me." ³ But Jonah rose up to flee to Tarshish from the presence of the Lord. So he went down to Joppa, found a ship which was going to Tarshish, paid the fare and went down into it to go with them to Tarshish from the presence of the Lord.

v.1—the word of the Lord came—Now it is just my opinion, many others may disagree, but I have a particular idea about this phrase in the Old Testament. I'm not sure how you envision what happens when a prophet hears from the Lord. Is it an audible voice? Does the prophet receive it in a dream or vision?

Because of my research[1] and belief that Jesus, the second person of the Godhead made Himself known in the Old Testament, I believe that when the Scripture says, the word of the Lord came, I believe it was an encounter with Christ in His pre-incarnate form.

Chad Bird writes, "This *dabar* [in Hebrew, the noun *dabar* [רָבָּד]] of the Lord is not a disembodied voice. He ushered Abram outside. Later, this *dabar* will touch Jeremiah's mouth (Jer. 1:4-9). This *dabar* would visit OT prophets and speak with them. They would not only hear but see the word of

---

[1] John M. Burris, The Visible Presence: Appearances of Christ in the Old Testament, (Houston: Worldwide Publishing, 2019.

the Lord. The one the OT calls the *dabar*, the NT will call the *Logos*."[2]

What must be clear is that this is a communication from the Lord to the prophet, no matter the delivery method.

v.2—arise, go to Nineveh and cry against it—The first thing to notice is this was unprecedented for a prophet to be called to go to the land they were prophesying against. Most of the time prophets of God were called to prophesy against God's people. This is especially remarkable given what we know about Nineveh. Not only was he to go there, but he was to "cry against it." Imagine God calling you to get on a plane, go to Afghanistan, walk into a Taliban encampment, and start calling out their wickedness. Talk about God telling someone something they don't want to hear! Jonah is the poster child for that kind of mission. His call to Nineveh, at least in Jonah's mind, was a death sentence.

v.3—But Jonah rose up to flee to Tarshish—Notice the directional language. God says, "Arise go to Nineveh." "Jonah rose up to flee." Where did he flee to? Tarshish. Tarshish is modern-day Spain. And you may not have the perspective of just how far that is.

---

[2] https://x.com/birdchadlouis/status/1831271845770772728

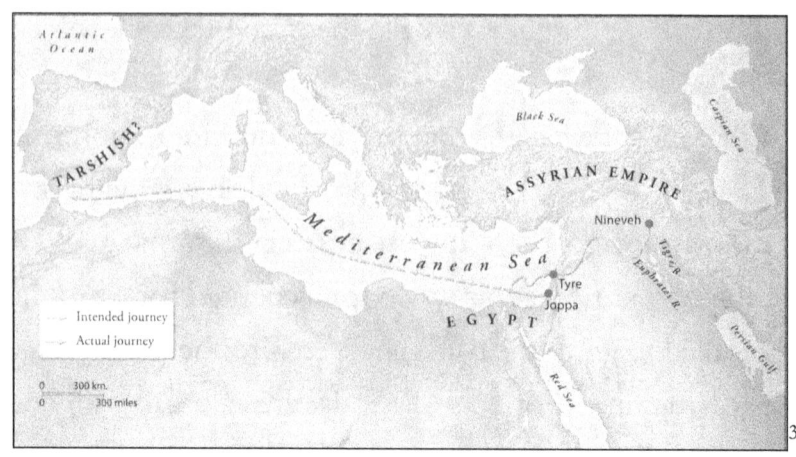

In Jonah's day, Tarshish was the farthest point West that the ancient world could have known. It was like the end of the world. So, Jonah is going as far as he possibly can away from God's instructions to him. Isaiah 66:19 gives us one more indication of why Jonah headed for Tarshish. *"I will set a sign among them and will send survivors from them to the nations: Tarshish, Put (PUHT), Lud (LUHD), Meshech (MEE—shek), Tubal (TYOO—buhl) and Javan (JAY—van), to the distant coastlands* **that have neither heard My fame nor seen My glory.***"*

Look at the last phrase of that sentence in v. 3, *"from the presence of the Lord."* The word "presence" is "face" in the Hebrew. Jonah is fleeing from the face of God.

---

[3] J. Daniel Hays and Tremper Longman III, The Message of the Prophets: A Survey of the Prophetic and Apocalyptic Books of the Old Testament, (Grand Rapids: Zondervan Academic, 2010), 300.

Have you ever wanted to get away from the Lord? I'm sure we've all experienced wanting to get away from our parents because we have either messed up big time or we know that we have disappointed them or as back in my day, about to get a "whoopin'."

But haven't we also just drifted away from the Lord? Have you ever just wished you could avoid His gaze, escape His conviction? Adam and Eve did, after they sinned, they thought they could cover their shame with fig leaves and hide behind the trees of the Garden. But they heard the sound of the Lord God walking in the Garden. The Hebrew word there means they heard the voice of the Lord walking in the garden. He was pursuing them.

Like Jonah, we often think we can hide from the Lord.

Jonah should have remembered what King David wrote in Psalm 139:7—10…

Where can I go from Your Spirit?
Or where can I flee from Your presence?
8 If I ascend to heaven, You are there;
If I make my bed in Sheol, behold, You are there.
9 If I take the wings of the dawn,
If I dwell in the remotest part of the sea,
10 Even there Your hand will lead me,
And Your right hand will lay hold of me.

So he went down to Joppa...—Notice again the Bible's use of language. The Lord told Jonah to arise, and he's done nothing but go down since then. His descent seems to reveal Jonah's desire to continue to flee from God's presence. But as the Lord Himself says in Jeremiah 23:23—24,

"Am I a God who is near," declares the Lord,
"And not a God far off?
24 "Can a man hide himself in hiding places
So I do not see him?" declares the Lord.
"Do I not fill the heavens and the earth?" declares the Lord.

We might think the obvious answer to the question of "Why didn't Jonah obey the Lord's command?" was to save his own skin. I would say that is indeed a part of it. But there is more to it than that. To really understand what's going on in Jonah's heart, we need to take a sneak peek at chapter 4:2, *"He prayed to the Lord and said, "Please Lord, was not this what I said while I was still in my own country? Therefore in order to forestall this I fled to Tarshish, for I knew that You are a gracious and compassionate God, slow to anger and abundant in lovingkindness, and one who relents concerning calamity.*

According to this, Jonah knew enough about God's mercy that if he went and cried out against Nineveh, they might just repent, and God would show them mercy. Jonah, however, didn't believe the Ninevites deserved the mercy of God. And we find here one of the many layers of this wonderful book.

The one who needed the mercy of God the most was not the city of Nineveh, but Jonah himself.

Matt Chandler says that whereas a good portion of the scriptures are a window into the heart of God, the book of Jonah is more like a mirror that reveals exactly who we are, and "We are Jonah."[4]

Even in these few short opening verses, we find that Jonah doesn't know as much about the mercy of God as he thinks he does. Throughout Jonah's journey, we are going to find that we don't know as much about God's mercy as we think we do.

The mercy of God is relentless. He is willing to pursue the objects of His love to the very deepest part of where we think we can hide from Him.

So I want to ask you, as I have been asking myself all summer while I've studied this, "Do you really believe that God is able to deliver you through your darkest moments?" and an even deeper question, "Will you hold on to Him, keep trusting Him, even if He doesn't do what you want Him to do?"

Maybe you worship the Lord out of habit or out of obligation, or maybe you're in church every Sunday…but

---

[4] https://www.thevillagechurch.net/resources/sermons/co-opted?mode=watch

if you were honest, you would rather run as far away from God as humanly possible. You don't like what He's told you. You don't like the circumstances in which you find yourself. You don't want to obey what He's called you to do, or you don't believe that there is enough mercy in the world to cover who you are and what you've done.

I challenge you to put Him to the test and see if His mercy is enough for whatever it is you are facing. Don't think the pew hides you from the gaze of the One who sees and knows all things.

If you are a believer in Jesus, a child of God, He will pursue that relationship with you to the ends of the earth.

If you have not yet trusted Jesus Christ as your Savior, He desires for you to know Him, He wants you to be saved! But I want to warn you, repeatedly in the Bible, He will let you run from Him if you continue to refuse Him.

From Prophet to Castaway
Jonah 1:4—16

How do we make sense of the storms that often hit our lives?

Sometimes we face storms because of our own sins.

Sometimes we face storms because of the choices of other people.

Sometimes we face storms because we live in a broken and fallen world.

What is God doing while we are drowning in our storms?

I heard a preacher once say in a sermon, "Every storm that comes into your life is brought by the hand of God." Something in my spirit just didn't sit right with that statement. I asked my pastor at the time, "Does that mean that God caused the disease that took my father's life?" "Does that mean that God is the cause of every storm we go through?"

Now that's been more than twenty-five years ago. I've learned a lot since then. I've endured several storms since then. I still don't agree with the statement.

Without a doubt, God is omniscient. He knows all things. But to say that He causes all things makes Him to be the author of chaos and evil and I don't think that is how the Bible describes God.

I believe that every storm that comes into our life passes through the hand of God and some of those storms are sent from His hand and some of them He allows us to endure for His ways, His purposes, and His plan.

Some may say that I'm haggling over semantics. Lord knows I am known to do that. But in a real sense how we answer that question matters to how we view who God is and how He interacts with us.

A.W. Tozer wrote, "What comes into our minds when we think about God is the most important thing about us."[5]

And what we believe about God matters when we are in the middle of a storm.

We face this conundrum right off the bat in **v.4**. "**The LORD hurled a great wind on the sea…**" The word hurled is used in other places in the OT for throwing a spear. It's hard to get around that one. The text is clear that the Lord caused the storm. But, why?

---

[5] A.W. Tozer, The Knowledge of the Holy, (San Francisco: Harper Collins Publishers, 1992), 1.

What do we know so far? God has called Jonah to go to Nineveh and "cry against it." Go to that wicked city and tell them just how wicked they are. God has given a tough assignment and Jonah wants no part of it. So, he boards a ship headed as far away as he could go, Tarshish. He's on the run from God, and as we saw in the last chapter, God is pursuing him.

Still in this first phrase, we see the word "**great**" again. This word or one of its forms is used over a dozen times in Jonah. Remember it's not a qualitative word. It's not referring to how wonderful something is, it is referring to how vast and powerful something is. The word "**wind**" is the same Hebrew word that is used for the spirit or the breath of God.

Then, you wouldn't think this was that significant, but in Hebrew, the wind is actually said to be "in" the sea, not on the sea. So, something is happening within the sea itself. This will be crucial to remember, so don't forget.

Then there was a "**great**", same word again "**storm**." The word storm is used as a whirlwind or a violent wind. "on the sea", again in the language it reads, "in the sea." Next, "so that the ship was about to **break up**." The word there is used for the shattering of the Ten Commandments, a bursting or imploding. In fact, the language personifies the boat as if the boat itself is pondering.

Now, I need to say a few things about the ancient Near Eastern concept of the sea and chaos. The Bible was not written to us, but it was written for us. In other words, we must understand the lens through which the people who first read the Bible in its original form would have understood it.

Just as we process things through the lens of our culture, the people of the ancient Near East had their own cultural lenses.

Before God called Abraham to begin a nation of a people who were to be God's own treasured possession, there were cultures and peoples who had developed their own systems of theology and ancient mythology. So, sometimes the Bible will use the motifs and imagery of the culture of the nations to communicate His truth.

In fact, sometimes the Bible uses the language and imagery of those "neighbors" of God's people to make light of them to show that Yahweh is the God above all other gods.

To the eastern mind, like that of Israel, the Sea, the wilderness, or darkness embodied the concept of chaos. Everything that was against God, against His plans and purposes was a part of this chaos.

But the Bible makes clear that there is nothing out of God's sovereign control, nothing beyond His watch.

So, in Genesis 1:2 when the Spirit is hovering above the waters, it almost seems like it is guarding what might be lurking there.

For many of the cultures that surrounded ancient Israel, the gods themselves were created in the sea and still lived within it. The sea monsters of Near Eastern mythology were thought to live just beneath the depths and would take any human's life whenever they pleased.

The sea was dangerous.

Look at **Genesis 1:21**

"God created the great sea monsters and every living creature that moves, with which the waters swarmed after their kind, and every winged bird after its kind; and God saw that it was good."

Because of this, it is not hard to explain the next verse.

v.5—The sailors became afraid—These would more than likely have been Phoenicians, a race of sea-faring people. In other words, there is not much they haven't seen on the sea.

and every man cried out to his god—If these were Phoenicians, they would have been a polytheistic people. They would have had multiple gods that they worshipped. So, they just cried out to whoever they thought could help them. You see, I think they knew that what they were dealing with was not just any storm at sea, but something supernatural.

they threw their cargo—the same word as hurled in v.4. This would have been their livelihood, their profits. This was probably a cargo vessel.

And where was Jonah during all this?

Jonah had gone below into the hold of the ship, lain down, and fallen asleep—Notice again Jonah's descent continues, below deck, lain down. We know what kind of sleep this is. Some of us have experienced it. It's the sleep of sorrow. Wanting so badly to escape reality for a time, we sometimes seek sleep despite what is happening around us.

v.6—The captain approached Jonah and said, "**Get up.**" Don't you know this was like the voice of God ringing in his sleeping ears, "Arise Jonah." Then the captain tells Jonah to call on his god.

v.7—The crew decides to cast lots. Now we don't know exactly what this would have been like. It could have been something like drawing straws or sometimes there were little stones, dark on one side and light on the other. If both were dark it was no, if both were light it was yes and if it was one of each it was indifferent. Nevertheless, the lot fell on Jonah.

v.8—They do a little investigative work. "What do you do?", "Where are you from?", "Who are your people?"

v.9—Look at what Jonah says, "**I am a Hebrew, and I fear the LORD GOD of Heaven who made the sea and the dry land.**" Now up to this point has Jonah's life looked like his confession? Does yours?

v.10—Then the men became extremely frightened—There is that word again, great. Its form lends that it be translated as "extremely", but it's the same word. Frightened? These are experienced sailors. Again, this is something extraordinary.

v.11—"What should we do to you?"—They realized that Jonah was the source, and he was the solution as well.

Also, **"the sea was becoming increasingly stormy."**

v.12—"Pick me up and throw me into the sea."—For the third time, we see the Hebrew word translated as hurled and throw. There is not much explanation for Jonah's response except that he would rather die than repent. To me, this is one of the saddest lines of text in the Bible.

Remember that the Sea was a representative of chaos. Many ancient cultures, including Israel, believed it was the gateway to the underworld.

But here is Jonah telling the sailors to throw him overboard.

Now let me stop here and say something. What Jonah is experiencing here is something that many people experience. It is emotions that are born from pity, self-hate, and the like. And I want to say what Jonah is proposing and what so many people have done is a permanent solution to a temporary problem.

And if at any time you are thinking that it would be just better for everyone if you weren't around. Please, please, I urge you to reconsider those thoughts. Every life is valuable to God and these kinds of thought patterns that one might think will bring wanted attention and relief from pain and anxiety only cause it to an even greater scale.

Talk to someone. It would be best to talk to a trusted friend or family member who can best provide accountability. But if you have those thoughts, please talk to someone.

v.13—The sailors were not ready to let Jonah give up. **"The men rowed desperately to return to land but they could not, for the sea was becoming even stormier against them."** The word for "rowed" there in the original language is a word that is best understood as "digging." This is something else you'll have to keep in mind as we move through the book of Jonah.

v.14—Now look at what the sailors did… **"They called on the LORD."** When you see the LORD in all caps in your Bible that means it is the covenant name of God, Yahweh. So, you have Gentile sailors now calling on the name of the God of Israel.

v.15—**"So they picked up Jonah, threw him into the sea, and the sea stopped its raging."** For the fourth time, the verb translated hurl or throw is used.

v.16—"Then the men feared the LORD greatly, and they offered a sacrifice to the LORD and made vows." It's interesting that the lives of Gentile sailors were changed but not the heart of the prophet of the Lord.

Let me see if I can kind of unpack all that we've heard. This is just one of the many things I've learned from studying the book of Jonah.

Yes, God called Jonah to go preach to the Ninevites. But I believe God had something more in mind than just the Ninevites. I think God, being outside of the concept of time, being the one who sees the end from the beginning, saw Jonah and the consequences of his decision to run away from Him and He decided to pursue the relationship with His wayward son to the point of hurling a storm onto the sea as a way of disciplining Jonah.

You see, God disciplines those He loves, the book of Hebrews reminds us of that. He scourges everyone He calls a son.[6]

And the reality is that if you are a child of God, He will allow you and yes, even sometimes send a storm to call you back into a relationship with Him. And guess what? Others may be swept up in that storm and they may feel the dread of that storm, or it may shake them to repentance.

J.I. Packer said it this way…

---

[6] Hebrews 12:6, NASB.

"Still he blesses those on whom He sets His love in a way that humbles them, so that all the glory may be His alone. Still He hates the sin of His people and uses all kinds of inward and outward pains and griefs to wean their hearts from compromise and disobedience. Still He seeks the fellowship of His people, and sends them both sorrows and joys in order to detach their love from other things and attach it to Himself."[7]

So, what is God doing while we are drowning in our storms?

He is as sovereign over the storm as He is over the chaos of the sea or the wilderness or of the darkness. He is right there in the midst of it with you.

Sometimes the storms in our life are God's way of beckoning us back to Himself. And if you are one who is running away from God and you're in a storm, He has a good reason for it and He will be with you all the way.

But I want to tell you, if you have not put your faith, in other words, entrusted your life to Jesus Christ, you may be caught up in the storms of life and there is no anchor for you, no rescue. Those Gentile sailors found that out, and they called on the LORD and He delivered them.

---

[7] J.I. Packer, Knowing God, (Downer's Grove: InterVarsity Press, 1993)

Whatever your excuse at this moment. Whatever reason you have for not trusting your life to Jesus Christ, His mercy is not only enough but more than you will ever need.

A Cry from the Depths
Jonah 1:17—2:10

Well, we left Jonah in the sea in the last chapter. I mentioned a couple of different things to keep in mind.

1.) The wind and the storm were not really "on" the sea, but "in" the sea.
2.) The picture of Ancient Cosmology. How the ancient people viewed the elements of the world.
3.) The word for "rowed" in 1:13 is best translated as "digging."

Now, I want to let you know that in this chapter there will be some things that will be different from anything you've ever heard before. But I want you to know, these are not just coming from my head or from a dream after something I ate. My intent is to stay right in the text and be as tied to the text as possible.

So, let's recap the scene. Jonah is inside a cargo vessel on the Mediterranean Sea headed for Tarshish, running from God. **Jonah 1:4** tells us that the Lord hurled (like a spear) a great wind **in** the sea that turned into a great storm **in** the sea. That was the reading of the text in Hebrew. Keep that in mind. It's as if the storm is coming from below the surface of the sea.

The sailors on the boat find out that Jonah is the cause of the storm. Jonah recommends that they throw him overboard. To try and keep that from happening they "rowed desperately." The word for "rowed" in **Jonah 1:13** is best translated as "digging." Of the eight times the word is used in Hebrew, seven times it is translated as "dig" and then there is this one time in Jonah where it is translated as "row." In fact, there is a different Hebrew word used for rowing in other passages of Scripture. So, we must ask, "if the word meant to dig, where are they and what are they digging in or through?"

Finally, the sailors hurl (like a spear) Jonah overboard. This is the same word that is used in v.4 where The Lord "hurled" a great wind in (on) the sea.

Now, before we get too far, it is important to have a basic understanding of Ancient Cosmology or how the Ancient Near East, the people during the Biblical times, saw the world. How the people of the Ancient Near East viewed the components of the earth is vastly different from our understanding. We have the benefit of technology to help us look into the heavens where we see vast galaxies beyond our own. Imagine how frightening the sea would have been for those who had no way to see below the surface of the water.

Consider this diagram from the Journal of Creation.

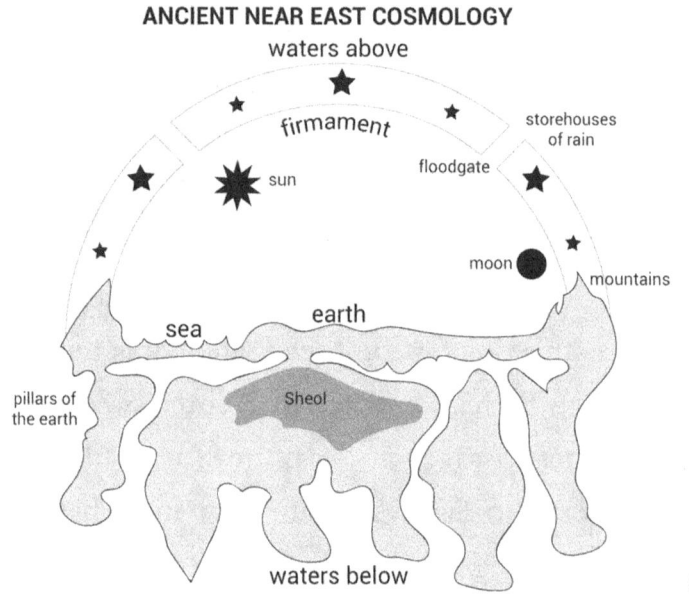

1.) Ancient people believed the sea was the gateway to Sheol which was the underworld, the realm of the dead in Old Testament thinking. They didn't have ways to see below the surface of the water or to drill below the earth. Could it be that the "digging' of the

---

[8] https://dl0.creation.com/articles/p140/c14041/after-Haarsma.jpg

sailors were actually digging into the walls of Sheol, the abode of the dead?

2.) Ancient people also believed the sea represented chaos, the forces that were against God. By the way, Revelation 21:1 says that in the new heaven and new earth there will no longer be any sea. Could this mean that there is no longer any chaos, no longer any place of mystery or lurking disaster in the new heaven and the new earth?

3.) This is all God's world. All His creation. None of this is outside of His control or domain.

Now we are ready for 1:17

And the Lord appointed—This will be the first of four elements of Creation that God appoints for Jonah. The other three are in Chapter 4. The word appointed means to number or to count or portion out something. God called up this part of His creation for His purpose.

a great fish—Now why is a whale in your head? Veggie Tales, a poster from Children's Sunday School, a book from your preschool days? Or is it from the KJV that uses the word whale in Matthew 12:40 when Jesus talks about Jonah?

Please understand this. The book of Jonah is not about a great fish, it is about a great God! The fish is not what matters in the text. The fact is we do not know for certain what exactly this was that God appointed to swallow Jonah. Now I will give you my opinion from the study of the text. But I read at least fifteen commentaries and watched five sermons and almost everyone has a different take on the fish.

My opinion is that this is not a whale. In fact, I don't think it looks like any kind of fish that we have ever identified. I think this is a sea monster. What kind of sea monster? I don't know. Maybe this Sea Monster retired to a lovely little loch in Scotland, like, I don't know…Loch Ness.

Let me explain my logic. Remember Genesis 1:21— "God created the great Sea Monsters." The Hebrew word for sea monsters is *tannin* which means a serpent.

But, if you were to look at the Greek translation of the Old Testament, the Greek word for Sea Monsters in Genesis 1:21 is *ketos* which is a word that means dragon.

Am I saying that this sea monster that swallows Jonah is a dragon? No. I'm saying it was a sea monster. It is probably unlike anything we have ever seen.

Genesis 1:21 in the Greek text "sea monsters" is translated as *ketos*.

Jonah 1:17 in the Greek text "a great fish" is translated as *ketos*.

Jonah 2:10 in the Greek text "fish" is translated as *ketos*.

Matthew 12:40, the NASB says sea monster, where the KJV says whale, the Greek word is *ketos*.

What this demonstrates is consistency. The translators of the Old Testament Hebrew, when they translated it into Greek (called the Septuagint) could have used one of several Greek words in Jonah 1:17. *Icthus* is a Greek word for fish. But they chose the word *ketos* for all three of those passages. The Jonah and Matthew passages are directly linked since Jesus is referring to the sign of Jonah.

Matthew 12:38—40

Then some of the scribes and Pharisees said to Him, "Teacher, we want to see a sign from You." ³⁹ But He answered and said to them, "An evil and adulterous generation craves for a sign; and yet no sign will be given to it but the sign of Jonah the prophet; ⁴⁰ for just as Jonah was three days and three nights in the belly of the sea monster, so will the Son of Man be three days and three nights in the heart of the earth.

The Pharisees are challenging the claims and work that Jesus has done. Jesus basically assures them that He is the Messiah by saying that the Kingdom of God has come upon them. Then they ask Him for a sign.

Here Jesus is referring to His death, His burial, and His resurrection.

So, for Jesus to use Jonah as a "sign" what does that mean?

The word in Greek there is *semeion* (sayMEHon) and this is what it means—a sign, mark, token, miracle with a spiritual end and purpose…miracles which lead to something out of and beyond themselves; fingermarks of God, **valuable not so much for what they are as for what they indicate of the grace and power of the Doer.**[9]

Here's what this means—Jesus is saying that the account of Jonah and the great fish is not so much about the whole fish swallowing and vomiting him out as it is about the fact that it is a miracle, the finger marks of God, and a signpost, a big glowing neon sign that says, "Look at God!"

Jonah and whatever sea monster/fish/Leviathan/whale that swallowed him is not the point! How did he survive three days in the belly of a sea monster? Not the point. What kind of species of fish would be big enough to swallow a man? Not the point, besides it's a miracle it doesn't have to be explained. The point is God. What did God do? And what did God do with Jonah? He brought him from death to life, just as Jesus would be brought from death to life.

Now to the text…

2:1—Then Jonah prayed to the Lord from the stomach of the fish—time order is hard to get in Jonah 2. All

---

[9] Olive Tree Bible Software, The Complete Word Study Dictionary of the New Testament, Greek word #4592.

we can know is that while Jonah was in the sea monster he prayed.

2:2—Look at the verbs in this prayer as we go. Watch for the tense.

I called out of my distress to the Lord

He answered me

I cried for help—from the depth of Sheol—the abode of the dead

You heard my voice

2:3—You had cast (notice he recognizes that God was the one who ultimately hurled him off the boat) me into the deep (another word for the underworld), into the heart (middle) of the seas (remember the ancient Israelite cosmology)

And the current **engulfed** me

Breakers and billows (waves and currents) **passed over** me

2:4—So I said, 'I **have been expelled** from Your sight (literally, before your eyes)

I need to stop here and comment. It was one thing for Jonah to get on a boat and want to be as far away from the face of God as possible. But then, he starts to feel it. He feels the separation and that's a whole different thing.

Nevertheless, **I will look** (future tense) again toward your holy temple

2:5—Water **encompassed** me to the point (literally, soul) of death

The great deep **engulfed** me

Weeds **were wrapped** around my head (the language of a burial shroud)

2:6—**I descended** to the roots of the mountains (cosmology—the deepest part of creation)

The earth with its bars (the underworld was thought to have bars or a door that locked to enclose it) **was** around me forever

But you **have brought** up my life from the pit (pit of death, Sheol, corruption), O Lord my God.

Notice the change in tense. For the first time, there is present tense. This is the point of recognition from Jonah that God has delivered him from Sheol, from death itself.

2:7—While I **was fainting** away, I **remembered** the Lord

And my prayer **came** to You, into Your holy temple

2:8—Those who **regard** vain idols **forsake** their faithfulness (*hesed*—mercy)

I think the meaning here is "Those who look to empty idols, give up hope for mercy."

2:9—But **I will sacrifice** to You with the voice of thanksgiving

That which **I have vowed I will pay** (he will perform his duty as a prophet)

Salvation **is** from the Lord

2:10—Then the Lord **commanded** the fish, and it vomited Jonah up onto dry land.

God is in control of the sea monster. Nothing is out of His control.

How do we make sense of Jonah's prayer from inside the belly of the sea monster?

Here is how I see it.

- Jonah is hurled into the sea by the sailors.
- As with everyone else at that time, the sea is chaos and the gateway to the underworld, therefore death.
- The ship is descending (with Jonah on it) and the sailors are digging into either the ocean floor or Sheol itself.
- Jonah begins to sink down to the depths continuing his descent that he began when he went down to Joppa.
- He is aware of all that happens to him as he descends to the roots of the mountains (v. 6a).
- Jonah dies and enters Sheol and there or on the way there, cries to the Lord for help.
- God appoints a sea monster to swallow Jonah and deliver him from Sheol.

- While in the belly of the sea monster, Jonah prays recounting his time in the deep, his time in Sheol, and his rescue from Sheol (v. 6b)
- And all along the entire journey from entering the sea until being vomited out on dry land, The Lord never left Jonah. Why? Because Jonah is His prophet? No, because Jonah is His child.

Listen, don't be distracted in Chapter 2 by the fish and Sheol and the underworld. Chapter 2 of Jonah is Jonah at the very lowest point of his life. And finally, he is broken. There is nothing left for him to hang onto, and he cried for help from the depth of Sheol. And at that lowest point God appoints a sea monster to come in and bring him back to life. And it is as if God is holding up that neon sign to us—"Pay attention! This is what I'll do for you too. But I will sacrifice the life of my very own Son so that you don't have to be separated from Me."

That is chapter 2 of Jonah.

In the last nine months, I've had my low points, some of the lowest points of my life. And yet God has been with me all along the way. I may not have always realized it, but He has been sustaining me all the way.

Sometimes God allows us to get to the low points in our lives to get our attention. He certainly did that with Jonah.

We are so easily distracted from a relationship with God. It seems we often pursue everything but Him. We chase after success, status, money, comfort, pleasure, our kids and all they do, acceptance, and approval. Think for a moment about what your thoughts and motivations have been centered on in the last month.

As I've said, the book of Jonah is like a mirror. It makes us see ourselves just like Jonah, a prideful, stubborn, selfish, arrogant individual who runs from God.

But the book of Jonah also acts as that glowing neon sign that says, "Look at God!" When we do, we see that God chases after Jonah even to the lowest point in his life. We see that God is relentless in His mercy. We see that the God who created the heavens, the land, and the sea and all that is in it, wants us to know Him.

This should be our Isaiah moment like when he had that glorious vision of the throne room of God and his response was, "Woe is me for I am ruined." He was broken, unable to stand because he saw how far his life had fallen from God's worth. He goes on and says, "For I am a man of unclean lips." His words betrayed the holiness of God. His life didn't match the pursuit of God that his calling suggested. And he said, "I live among a people of unclean lips." Seemingly, everyone around him was going about their lives chasing whatever pleased or satisfied them.

But he declares, "For my eyes have seen the King, the Lord Almighty."[10]

When he saw the brilliance, the beauty, the tenderness, and mercy of the God who created him, nothing else compared. Oh, to live every moment in that realization. But we must first be broken.

---

[10] Isaiah 6, NASB.

The Great City Repents
Jonah 3:1—10

Well, we've left Jonah on the land somewhere having been vomited out of the sea monster onto dry land.

We don't know where he has been expelled. Is it back near Joppa? Is it on the way to Nineveh? Or is it at some other point between Joppa and Tarshish?

We don't know for certain. But the text seems to indicate that the storm in the sea happened rather quickly after they set sail. In my opinion, the ship had not sailed very far. Of course, we cannot account for how far the sea monster traveled or in which direction during the time Jonah was in its belly.

Nevertheless, Jonah is now on dry land, smelling like yesterday's Long John Silvers and that's where we pick up the text in 3:1.

¹ Now the word of the Lord came to Jonah the second time, saying—Jonah didn't obey the first time the word of the Lord came to him, but the Lord calls to him yet again.

² **"Arise, go to Nineveh the great city and proclaim to it the proclamation which I am going to tell you."** – The calling is similar but not the exact message Jonah first received. This time God just tells him, "Just say what I tell you to."

³ **So Jonah arose and went to Nineveh according to the word of the Lord. Now Nineveh was an exceedingly great city, a three days' walk.**—We see a different result so far this time, Jonah arose and went to Nineveh.

an exceedingly great city—This is tricky. And I don't really understand why translators ignore the Hebrew word here that is staring them in the face. Exceedingly great city—*ir gadol elohim*—Literally the phrase means "a great city to God." I believe the sense we are to get from this is that Nineveh is an important city to God. Why? I think the answer lies in the last verse of the book, **4:11**. *"Should I not have compassion on Nineveh, the great city in which there are more than 120,000 persons who do not know the difference between their right and left hand, as well as many animals?"*

God sees and cares for the lost souls of all His creation and those in Nineveh were most certainly lost.

This will become a bit clearer as we study Chapter 4, but in Jonah 4:2, Jonah's own words declare that God is a *"gracious and compassionate God, slow to anger and abundant in lovingkindness, and one who relents concerning calamity."*

a three days' walk—Almost every scholar agrees that this does not mean it took Jonah three days to get to Nineveh (even though that is how we would say it). What it meant is that Nineveh is so large it would take three days to walk through the city.

⁴Then Jonah began to go through the city one day's walk; and he cried out and said, "Yet forty days and Nineveh will be overthrown."

one day's walk—It could be that Jonah only went as far into Nineveh as one day's walk, or not all the way through. Jonah may have found a nice park bench and sat down, maybe a fountain where he could dry to rid himself of the stench of the sea monster. One—third of the way through the city. Or, the Hebrew language could be constructed in such a way as to imply, "he just began making his way through the city, a single day's journey when he proclaimed."

Yet forty days and Nineveh will be overthrown—This may be the strangest part of the chapter: eight words in our English translation and only five words in the Hebrew. Most prophets have whole books worth of things to proclaim. We are left with the question, "Is this really exactly what God told Jonah to say?" We have no way of knowing.

But three clues give us a strong indication that there may have been more.

1. We know that Jonah is reluctant, to say the least about His mission to the people of Nineveh. He doesn't want to go, and he doesn't want them to repent.
2. The usual preamble to any proclamation that a prophet makes is, "Thus saith The Lord!" or "This is what Yahweh says!" That is absent here.
3. Again, the usual prophetic method indicated either a stated cause of impending doom or a path of deliverance based on the response of the recipient of the prophecy. There are neither of those things here that we know of.

overthrown—This is the Hebrew word (*hapak*), and it means to turn over. The first use of this word was in the account of the destruction of Sodom and Gomorrah in Genesis 19:21 and is used 4 times in vv.21—29.

Genesis 19:29

"Thus it came about, when God destroyed the cities of the valley, that God remembered Abraham, and sent Lot out of the midst of the overthrow, when He overthrew the cities in which Lot lived."

So, the intended feel of this word from Jonah was destruction. Forty days and Nineveh will be overthrown. What should forty days call to mind? Not to make too much out of a number, but, in the Bible, forty is seen as the number of testing and trials or trouble and hardship. In the days of Noah, forty days and forty nights of rain, Moses on Mt. Sinai for forty days, forty years the Israelites wandered in the wilderness, forty days Jesus was tempted by Satan in the wilderness.

Whether God specifically told Jonah to say nothing but those words or not, the original instruction from God was for Jonah to cry against Nineveh because of their wickedness.

But there is also another shade of meaning to this word "overthrown." It also means to change, to transform, like turning over a new leaf.

How do we determine which use of the word is being used? Context. Knowing what we do about Jonah, it seems that, coming from him, he means destruction. "Forty days and you're done for!" But knowing what we do about God…remember relentless mercy…despite Jonah's disposition, God could be saying through Jonah, forty days and Nineveh will be transformed.

Which is it? I think we must live with the tension. It could be both. Certainly, Jonah meant destruction and the

Ninevites understood the proclamation to be destruction. But God may have something else in mind.

Look at the result of this five-word sermon.

⁵ Then the people of Nineveh believed in God; and they called a fast and put on sackcloth from the greatest to the least of them.

The most amazing thing happens! The people of Nineveh respond to Jonah's message. They called a fast, put on sackcloth which represents humility. I mean Jonah has got to be looking around, going, "What is happening?" Remember, he does not want Nineveh to repent and suddenly, it's the greatest revival in all of history!

Now I just want to throw this out there as a possibility. We cannot know for sure. But word must have spread that this prophet from Israel was vomited up from a sea monster. If so, remember that one of the gods of the Ninevites was Dagon, the fish god, half man and half god. They also believed that the seas were the home of their gods. And so, if this prophet's God has overcome the sea monster and the sea, maybe we had better humble ourselves before Jonah's God.

⁶ When the word reached the king of Nineveh, he arose from his throne, laid aside his robe from him, covered *himself* with sackcloth and sat on the ashes.

Here is the King of Nineveh, and he gets word second-hand. He gets wind of it. He takes off his robes of royalty. This would be extremely uncharacteristic of a King. He puts on sackcloth and sits in ashes. Sitting in ashes is to sit in the earth. It is a posture that represents death. So, we have a king who humbles himself and takes on the posture of death.

⁷ He issued a proclamation and it said, "In Nineveh by the decree of the king and his nobles: Do not let man, beast, herd, or flock taste a thing. Do not let them eat or drink water.

The people are way ahead of the king. They have already called a fast and put on sackcloth. But the king makes it official.

⁸ But both man and beast must be covered with sackcloth; and let men call on God earnestly that each may turn from his wicked way and from the violence which is in his hands.

So, you can imagine Jonah walking through Nineveh and at every house the family is out trying to get the livestock in sackcloth. It must have been quite a sight.

Look at the second part of the verse.

that each may turn—Hebrew word *shuv* means just the act of turning around, directional.

wicked way—Wicked is the Hebrew word *raah*, which means evil. There was some recognition that their ways were not in line with this god.

violence—This is the Hebrew word *chamas*. Not HAMAS, like the terror group, that's an acronym. But Nineveh was known as the City of Blood. Remember the violent nature of the city.

⁹ Who knows, God may turn and relent and withdraw His burning anger so that we will not perish."

The king seems to think that if they "turn" (*shuv*) from their evil, God may just "turn" (*shuv*) Himself and relent (*naham*).

relent—(*naham*) Throughout the Bible this Hebrew word is used and translated in a variety of ways. Comfort, console, grieve, express sympathy, but also, change one's mind.

This word should cause us a bit of heartburn. How can God relent? Can God change His mind if He is sovereign and all-knowing?

Look at this passage after Saul is removed from authority as King of Israel.

1 Samuel 15:28—29

"So Samuel said to him, "The Lord has torn the kingdom of Israel from you today and has given it to your neighbor, who is better than you. ²⁹ Also the Glory of Israel will not lie or (naham) **change His mind;** *for He is not a man that He should (naham)* **change His mind."**

Turn—(Hebrew word *shuv*) A literal turning of direction

Relent/Change His mind—(Hebrew word *naham*) to be sorry, to pity, to comfort, to avenge

I believe that when *naham* refers to God, it is to be understood that although God can express grief or remorse, He will never change His mind aimlessly. And even if He turns, or changes His mind, it is never contrary to His covenant promises.

Tim Mackie said, "The word *naham* invites us into the deep mystery of the creator's purpose to genuinely partner with humans in the course of history."[11]

All through the Bible God uses frail and faulty people to accomplish His purpose. That is messy. He must deal with our emotions and willful decisions.

Here is what all this means…Why would God change His mind about destroying the people of Nineveh? If they did indeed repent, He is bound by His covenant loyalty. He is true to Himself and His character and nature. He cannot lie or change His covenant loyalty. What is His covenant loyalty?

Jonah 4:2—Jonah affirms what he knows to be true about God and declares that this is the reason why he didn't want to go to Nineveh in the first place.

He prayed to the Lord and said, "Please Lord, was not this what I said while I was still in my own country? Therefore, in

---

[11] https://bibleproject.com/classroom/jonah

order to forestall this **I fled to Tarshish, for I knew** *that You are a gracious and compassionate God, slow to anger and abundant in* **lovingkindness (hesed, covenant loyalty, relentless mercy)**, *and one who* **relents** *(naham) concerning calamity.*

God will be true to His relentless mercy. Jonah knew this about God. He knew that if God showed Himself to the people of Nineveh and they turned and repented of their evil, God would inevitably show them His relentless mercy.

In this way, we see the beautiful paradox of Jonah 3:4. Listen to it from each perspective…

Jonah—"Yet forty days and Nineveh will be overturned (destroyed)."

God—"Yet forty days and Nineveh will be overturned (changed)."

This shows that God will be true to His character and His purpose. Yes, He involves flawed human beings in the process. But His relentless mercy triumphs even our failures.

Look at how the chapter ends.

¹⁰ When God saw their deeds, that they turned (shuv) from their wicked way, then God relented (naham) concerning the calamity which He had declared He would bring upon them. And He did not do *it.*

Did God change from His character and His covenant loyalty? On the contrary, He put His covenant loyalty on full display.

Some of us are in the place of Jonah, bitter, angry, stiff-necked. We want our way rather than God's way.

Some of us are in the place of the people of Nineveh, full of sin, wicked in our thoughts and ways, and enemies of God.

And yet for all of us, there is One who is ready to stand in our place and stretch out His hands upon a Roman cross to take our punishment.

Because make no mistake. God possesses a burning anger toward sin and there is the calamity of the justice and wrath of God that must be expressed upon those who are His enemies.

The good news, the gospel is that God poured out His burning anger toward sin upon His only Son, Jesus Christ, who would be the recipient of that justice, wrath, and punishment. The Bible says He became sin for us.

2 Corinthians 5:21

He made Him who knew no sin to be sin on our behalf, so that we might become the righteousness of God in Him.

And this God of relentless mercy, makes the same offer to us as He did to the Ninevites. If we turn (*shuv*) from our wicked ways and seek God's forgiveness through Jesus Christ, He will (*naham*) relent from condemning us to the life and eternal death that our sin deserves and grant us the gift of eternal life in Jesus Christ.

There may be some of us who have turned from our sin time after time by saying, "God, please forgive me, I never want to do that again." And we may have turned away from sin for the moment, but we've never turned our hearts toward Jesus Christ.

Maybe today is the day that for the first time you not only turn away from your sin and your rebellious heart, but you walk toward Jesus. Put your full trust in Him. Ask Him to overturn your heart so that you begin to walk in His way.

I believe what you will find when you do is relentless mercy. You will find the kind of love that you never knew existed, stronger than any human emotion.

The Reflection of the Heart
Jonah 4:1—11

Mirror, Mirror on the wall, who is the fairest one of all? In Snow White, the evil Queen consults her magic mirror to make sure that she is the most beautiful in all the land. In the original, she said, "Magic mirror on the wall, who is the fairest one of all? And there was something inside the mirror, the queen called it a slave that spoke to her.

Well as we close out the book of Jonah, we are going to consult the Word of God as our mirror, our measure of how our lives reflect the character of Christ. We will see Jonah as completely self-centered and self-righteous. And as we do, we will hold the text up as a mirror and see if we have those same tendencies.

In the last chapter, Nineveh, the great city "to" God, experienced an incredible movement of repentance. This widespread repentance resulted in God relenting from bringing calamity on the city, or from destroying the city.

v.1—But it greatly displeased Jonah, and he became angry—Jonah's reaction should evoke some feeling on our part. Jonah, how can you be angry that the Ninevites repented, and God showed His mercy?

But listen to the Hebrew words in v.1—And it was evil to Jonah, a great evil, and there was heat-anger to him. The word "displeased" is *Raah*, which is a word often translated as evil.

Jonah was upside down in his thinking. He had honestly arrived at the belief that God should punish evil or wickedness at any cost. No matter what. So, to Jonah, it didn't matter one bit that the Ninevites repented, and turned from their evil. They didn't deserve God's mercy.

In v. 2 Jonah prays to the Lord.

v.2—He prayed to the Lord and said, 'Please Lord, was this not what I said while I was still in my own country? I want to draw your attention back to the book of Exodus chapter 14 because this is one of those hyperlinks that I've mentioned before. Words or phrases in the text that should draw your mind to other portions of the Bible.

Exodus 14:10—13

[10] As Pharaoh drew near, the sons of Israel looked, and behold, the Egyptians were marching after them, and they became very

frightened; so, the sons of Israel cried out to the Lord. **¹¹** *Then they said to Moses, "Is it because there were no graves in Egypt that you have taken us away to die in the wilderness? Why have you dealt with us in this way, bringing us out of Egypt?* **¹² Is this not the word that we spoke to you in Egypt, saying, 'Leave us alone that we may serve the Egyptians'? For it would have been better for us to serve the Egyptians than to die in the wilderness."** **¹³** *But Moses said to the people, "Do not fear! Stand by and see the salvation of the Lord which He will accomplish for you today; for the Egyptians whom you have seen today, you will never see them again forever."*

So, Jonah's words here in v.2 are parallels to the words of the Israelites as they fled Egypt. Pharoah's army is on their heels and in those moments of fear, they are not convinced of God's provision for them. And that's the parallel, that plays itself out in the remainder of Jonah.

Therefore, in order to forestall this, I fled to Tarshish—finally, he admitted what he did. What did he want to forestall? God's mercy to the Ninevites.

for I knew that You are a gracious and compassionate God,—the adjectives gracious and compassionate are almost always linked together in describing the nature and character of God.

slow to anger—this is a Hebrew idiom that is literally, "long of nostrils."

- **and abundant in lovingkindness, and one who relents concerning calamity.**—The word lovingkindness, *hesed* in Hebrew, has no adequate English word that captures its meaning. We use the words mercy or grace to try and capture this aspect of God's character.

Jonah knew about God. He was a prophet, in the tradition of Moses, He knew the Torah. Yet here he is angry and thinking that God's mercy is a great evil. How does someone who knows Yahweh, knows His word, turn out to be this way?

Hold up your mirror.

v.3—Therefore now, O Lord, please take my life from me, for death is better to me than life."—How out of touch with reality has Jonah become? Because God showed mercy to a people that he thinks don't deserve it, he's ready to die. Get ready to hold up that mirror again. I submit to you that there are ideals, notions, and beliefs if you want to go that far, that are not at all Biblical, doctrinal, or even reasonable that we hold fast to as if they are inscribed by the finger of God. We easily become the arbiters of righteousness for our own self-determined truth.

Look how God responds.

v.4—The Lord said, "Do you have good reason to be angry?"—You need to hear it in the Hebrew… And Yahweh said, "Is it good that there is heat-anger to you?"

Here we need to do another hyperlink.

Genesis 4:3—6

"So, it came about in the course of time that Cain brought an offering to the Lord of the fruit of the ground. ⁴ Abel, on his part also brought of the firstlings of his flock and of their fat portions. And the Lord had regard for Abel and for his offering; ⁵ but for Cain and for his offering He had no regard. **So, Cain became very angry** *and his countenance fell.* **⁶ Then the Lord said to Cain, "Why are you angry?** *And why has your countenance fallen?"*

Do you see the parallel? Cain had an ideal, notion, or belief in his mind that God should have regard for his offering. However, the truth was that it was not an offering that God saw as acceptable. So, Cain became angry. Same words as in Jonah.

Genesis 4:7—15

If you do well, will not your countenance be lifted up? And **if you do not do well, sin is crouching at the door;**

and its desire is for you, but you must master it."
⁸ Cain told Abel his brother. And it came about when they were in the field, that **Cain rose up against Abel his brother and killed him.** *⁹ Then the Lord said to Cain, "Where is Abel your brother?" And he said, "I do not know.* **Am I my brother's keeper?"** *¹⁰ He said, "What have you done? The voice of your brother's blood is crying to Me from the ground. ¹¹ Now you are cursed from the ground, which has opened its mouth to receive your brother's blood from your hand. ¹² When you cultivate the ground, it will no longer yield its strength to you; you will be a vagrant and a wanderer on the earth." ¹³ Cain said to the Lord, "My punishment is too great to bear! ¹⁴ Behold, You have driven me this day from the face of the ground; and from Your face I will be hidden, and I will be a vagrant and a wanderer on the earth, and whoever finds me will kill me."¹⁵ So the Lord said to him, "Therefore whoever kills Cain, vengeance will be taken on him sevenfold."* **And the Lord appointed a sign for Cain, so that no one finding him would slay him.** *¹⁶* **Then Cain went out from the presence of the Lord, and settled in the land of Nod, east of Eden.**

We have already seen in chapter 1 that Jonah fled to Tarshish "from the presence of the Lord."

Look at what Jonah does in verse 5.

v.5—Then Jonah went out from the city and sat east of it—just like Cain.

There he made a shelter for himself and sat under it in the shade until he could see what would happen in the city—The Cain parallel continues.

Genesis 4:17

Cain had relations with his wife and she conceived, and gave birth to Enoch; and **he built a city***, and called the name of the city Enoch, after the name of his son.*

The Lord had appointed a sign for Cain to keep him from harm. Yet here he decides to create his own protection in the way of a city.

The word for shelter in Jonah 4:5 is *sukkah*. That may be familiar to you because that's what the Israelites were instructed to build during the Feast of Tabernacles which is also called Sukkot.

During Sukkot, the Israelites celebrated God's continued provision for them in the current harvest and remembered His provision and protection during the forty years in the wilderness. So, people would build these little tent shelters and would live in them for a week to remind them that it is God who takes care of them.

But Jonah made a shelter for himself…until he could see what would happen to Nineveh. He still was waiting for them to get what he thought they were due. Justice. But because of their repentance, God showed mercy.

v.6—So the Lord God appointed a plant and it grew up over Jonah to be a shade over his head—Remember the Lord appointed a sign for Cain? Here he appoints a sign for Jonah in a plant. This is the second time God has appointed something for Jonah. And every time He does it will be an attempt to turn Jonah's heart.

to deliver him from his discomfort—Discomfort is the word *Raah*.

And Jonah was extremely happy about the plant—Why was Jonah suddenly happy? Because he thought that finally, God was coming around to his way of thinking. God was doing something for him now. And he didn't realize God had been doing something for him all along the way.

Hold up your mirror!

Look what God does next.

v.7—But God appointed a worm when dawn came the next day and it attacked the plant and it withered—This is the third thing that God has appointed. And you might think here that God is just messing with him. But I believe God is trying to make Jonah see that he didn't have to trust in only what he could do for himself.

Hold up your mirror again.

v.8—When the sun came up God appointed a scorching east wind, and the sun beat down on Jonah's

head so that he became faint and begged with *all* his soul to die, saying, "Death is better to me than life."—The final element of creation that God appoints is an east wind. We are to assume that the east wind also carries away the tent shelter Jonah had built leaving Jonah with nothing but himself against the backdrop of a city that still has not been destroyed.

This may have been the undoing of Jonah. We don't really know. But his selfishness and self-righteousness may have prevented him from surrendering to God.

v.9—Then God said to Jonah, "Do you have good reason to be angry about the plant?"—God brought up the plant. You'd think there would be more important questions that God might ask. But really the root of the plant experience revealed Jonah's real problem. Would Jonah trust what he could do or what God could provide? His own ingenuity, his own ideals, his own presuppositions about how God reacts and responds to His own creation, or trust that God knows what He's doing.

When what we know about God is confronted with our own selfish desires, and our own self-righteousness, our inclination is for us to think that our own desires to be the things that God should be doing. When that happens, we put ourselves in the place of God.

Jacques Ellul said it this way, "[Jonah] creates his own domain in the shade where he will be at peace according to his own measure, just as Christians try to make a church according to their own measure…full of intentions which are good and effective and well-constructed, but which are only a fresh demonstration of their autonomy in relation to God."[12]

And he said, "I have good reason to be angry, even to death."—My translation. "I don't want your help. You are not being just." Or better yet, "You should be doing it this way, my way."

Anyone need to hold up their mirror?

v.10—11—Then the Lord said, "You had compassion on the plant for which you did not work and *which you did not cause to grow, which came up overnight and perished overnight*. Should I not have compassion on Nineveh, the great city in which there are more than 120,000 persons who do not know *the difference* between their right and left hand, as well as many animals?"

The Lord is saying to Jonah, "You had compassion on a plant that you had nothing to do with, but you couldn't find compassion for the people who don't know Me?"

And the book just ends that way. No resolve. No nice tidy package of a story with a happy ending. We don't know

---

[12] James Montgomery Boice, <u>The Minor Prophets: An Expositional Commentary</u>, Vol.1 (Grand Rapids: Baker Books, 1983), 308.

what happened to Jonah. But the question is left not only for Jonah to ponder but for us as well.

Do we really understand the relentless mercy of God? Or do we have our own ideas about how God ought to act, how the church ought to be, and anybody who doesn't fit that ideal, they don't get my compassion?

We've seen Jonah embodied in Cain. But there is someone else in the Bible like Jonah. Jonah is like the older brother in the parable of the prodigal son.

You remember that one. A man had two sons, one wanted his inheritance early so he could go live "*la vida loca*", his best life, and fulfill **his** desires. He ends up in poverty living in a pig pen and decides to crawl back home to his father. His father embraces him, welcomes him, throws a party for the neighborhood, and kills a nice fat calf to feast on. But then there is the older brother, the one who stayed behind and worked hard. The one who had his own ideas about his younger brother, just like Cain. Listen to how he responds to his father.

Luke 15:28—32

"But he became angry and was not willing to go in; and his father came out and began pleading with him. ²⁹ But he answered and said to his father, 'Look! For so many years I have been serving you and I have never neglected a command

> *of yours; and yet you have never given me a young goat, so that I might celebrate with my friends;* ³⁰ *but when this son of yours came, who has devoured your wealth with prostitutes, you killed the fattened calf for him.'* ³¹ *And he said to him, 'Son, you have always been with me, and all that is mine is yours.* ³² *But we had to celebrate and rejoice, for this brother of yours was dead and has begun to live and was lost and has been found.'"*

Do you remember the primary audience of that little lesson parable? Tax collectors and sinners and Pharisees and scribes. These groups represented the two characters in the parable. The tax collectors and sinners were the younger brother who repented and the Pharisees and scribes were the older brother, the self—righteous one.

Jesus possessed the unique ability to teach, in one story, a multitude of lessons. The parable of the lost son was preceded by the parable of the lost coin and the lost sheep. On one hand, Jesus declared that there were lost people all around. Jesus' heart and mission was to seek and save the lost.[13]

We pass lost people every day, we are in the grocery store with them, they serve us our food at restaurants, they live in our neighborhoods, they work at desks near us. Penn Jillette of the magic team Penn and Teller said, "How much

---

[13] Luke 19:10, NASB.

do you have to hate somebody to believe everlasting life is possible and not tell them that?"[14]

Hold up your mirrors once again!

On the other hand, Jesus' parable was a stark warning to the very people who should have joined Him in pointing the lost to life in Him. The scribes and Pharisees were so focused on adhering to the letter of the Law that they could not recognize the Messiah when He was right in front of them.

What confronts us in Jonah 4 is the mirror of the Word of God and more than that the King of Kings, the Lord Jesus Christ. And it is as if we stand with Him face to face and go, "Meh, I can do better."

This is the Lord of Glory. The One Isaiah described as "This One who is majestic in His apparel, marching in the greatness of His strength, speaking in righteousness, mighty to save."

Let me close with this poem by Thomas John Carlisle

And Jonah stalked
to his shaded seat
and waited for God
to come around
to his way of thinking.

---

[14] https://www.thegospelcoalition.org/blogs/justin-taylor/how-much-do-you-have-to-hate-somebody-to-not-proselytize/

And God is still waiting
for a host of Jonahs
in their comfortable houses
to come around
to his way of loving.[15]

---

[15] Thomas John Carlisle, <u>You! Jonah!</u>, (Grand Rapids: Wm. B. Eerdmans, 1974), 64.

One more thing…

One of the most amazing things about God is that He is so magnificent and complex but, at the same time, so simple that a child can believe in Him. After all, belief is the only requirement for having a personal relationship with God. So, I want to just lay out a few truths for you. These truths are not just random facts. They are truths about a person, a person who created you, loves you, and wants you to spend eternity in the place He has created for you.

- **God has created us and the world around us. Thus, we are accountable to Him.**

    "God created man in His own image, in the image of God He created him; male and female He created them."— Genesis 1:27

- **Every one of us is a sinner. We break God's laws.**

  "For all have sinned and fall short of the glory of God,"—Romans 3:23

- **If we remain in our sin, without someone to rescue us, we will spend eternity separated from God.**

  "For the wages of sin is death, but the free gift of God is eternal life in Christ Jesus our Lord."—Romans 6:23

- **God sent His Son, Jesus Christ, into the world to rescue us, die for our sins, and make us right with God.**

  "For God so loved the world, that He gave His only begotten Son, that whoever believes in Him shall not perish, but have eternal life."—John 3:16

- **When we put our trust in Jesus' sacrifice as the only way we can be right with God, and He promises to give us eternal life.**

  "If you confess with your mouth Jesus as Lord, and believe in your heart that God raised Him from the dead, you will be saved."—Romans 10:9

Relentless Mercy

If you have never understood these truths, you have an opportunity to make the greatest decision you could ever make. By the death, burial, and resurrection of Jesus Christ, God has offered you to know Him personally and spend eternal life in Heaven. Will you believe in Him? Will you put your trust in Jesus to save you from your sin?

The good news is that you don't have to get your life straightened out before you make this decision. God accepts you as you are. But please understand, that if you really do believe in Him and put your trust in Him, He will change you. He will make you into a different person. The Bible says in 2 Corinthians 5:17, "*Therefore if any man is in Christ, he is a new creature; the old things passed away; behold, new things have come.*"

To make this life-changing decision, it is as simple as asking. Right now, you can pray something like this…

> *God, I know that there have been many times that I have broken your law, I am a sinner. I understand that my sin needs forgiveness. I know that the only way for me to be forgiven is to believe that Jesus died so that I could live. So, now I put my trust in Jesus. I believe that He died for my sin. And now I want Him to make me new. I want Him to be my Lord and my Savior. In Jesus' name, Amen*

The words that you say are not as important as the attitude of your heart. If you put your trust in Jesus, He will save you, completely and forever. Following Jesus and getting to know Him will be the most fulfilling journey you could ever embark upon. He is worth trusting.

For Further Study

The Bible Project—Jonah and the…Chaos Dragon? https://bibleproject.com/podcast/jonah-and-chaos-dragon/

Boice, James Montgomery—<u>The Minor Prophets: An Expositional Commentary, Vol. 1 Hosea—Jonah</u>, (Grand Rapids: Baker Books, 1983)

Carlisle, Thomas John—<u>You! Jonah!</u>, (Grand Rapids: Wm Eerdmans, 1968)

Cary, Phillip—<u>Brazos Theological Commentary on the Bible: Jonah</u>, (Grand Rapids: Brazos Press, 2008)

Exell, Joseph S.—<u>Practical Truths from Jonah</u>, (Grand Rapids: Kregel Publications, 1982)

Heiser, Michael-—The Ancient's Guide to the Galaxy: How the Israelites Viewed God and the Universe https://www.logos.com/grow/ancients-guide-galaxy-israelites-viewed-god-universe/

Heiser, Michael—Jonah and the Chaos Dragon
https://nakedbiblepodcast.com/wp-content/uploads/2020/11/NB-347-Transcript.pdf

Mackie, Tim—The Bible Project Classroom Jonah Unit (45 Sessions)
https://bibleproject.com/classroom/jonah/sessions/1

MacArthur, John—Jonah & Nahum, (Los Angeles: The Master's Seminary Press, 2024)

Magonet, Jonathan—Form and Meaning: Studies in Literary Techniques in The Bok of Jonah, (Sheffield: Almond Press, 1983)

Martin, Hugh—Geneva Series of Commentaries: Jonah, (East Peoria: Versa Press, 2021)

Noegel, Scott B.—Jonah and Leviathan: Inner—Biblical Allusions and the Problem with Dragons
https://faculty.washington.edu/snoegel/PDFs/articles/noegel-jonah-2015.pdf

Ogilvie, Lloyd J.—Mastering the Old Testament: Hosea, Joel, Amos, Obadiah, Jonah, (Dallas: Word Publishing, 1990)

Overdun, Jan—Adventures of a Deserter, (Grand Rapids: William B. Eerdmans, 1965)

Sasson, Jack M.—Jonah: A New Translation with Introduction, Commentary and Interpretations, (New Haven: Yale University Press, 1990)

Wiersbe, Warren—Be Amazed: Restoring an Attitude of Wonder and Worship Selected Minor Prophets, (Wheaton: Victor Books, 1996)

Youngblood, Kevin—Jonah: A Discourse Analysis of the Hebrew Bible, vol. 28 Zondervan Exegetical Commentary on the Old Testament (Grand Rapids: Zondervan Academic, 2013)

www.ingramcontent.com/pod-product-compliance
Lightning Source LLC
LaVergne TN
LVHW010606070526
838199LV00063BA/5092